The
BASICS

*Get in the*

# GAME

basics of christian service

Leader Guide

Clayton Oliphint
*and*
Mary Brooke Casad

Abingdon Press
Nashville

**Get in the Game**
**Basics of Christian Service**
**Leader Guide**

*This book is printed on elemental, chlorine-free paper.*
ISBN 978-1-5018-1319-1

16 17 18 19 20 21 22 23 24 25 — 10 9 8 7 6 5 4 3 2 1
MANUFACTURED IN THE UNITED STATES OF AMERICA

# CONTENTS

# INTRODUCTION

Every follower of Jesus is faced with a moment of decision: do we stay on the sidelines or get in the game? Jesus indicates in the Gospels that he came that we might have abundant life and that the best way to find that life is not through getting everything we want but through learning to love God by serving others. In following Christ, we are challenged to use our gifts to be a blessing to the world that God so loves. Many people looking for fulfillment in life do not understand this. They somehow have bought into the notion that the way to be fulfilled in life is to acquire more possessions, make more money, and have everything you want. But Jesus points us in a different direction. For Christians, getting in the game is about those daily decisions to live selflessly, opening ourselves for God to use us in service.

The chapters in *Get in the Game* are designed to challenge and encourage us to put faith in action. In Chapter 1, we talk about learning the basics of loving God and neighbor. In Chapter 2, we are striving to get in "the zone," that is, to be in sync with what God desires, allowing God to transform us into the servants God wants us to be. In Chapter 3, we focus on living out God's will for our lives through living a joy-filled life, a life of prayer, and a life of gratitude for our many blessings. Chapter 4 challenges us to get "all in" in serving God, with a focus on living a generous life.

This four-session study is ideal for discussion groups, such as Sunday school classes and other small groups. Before the first session, each participant will need a copy of the *Get in the Game* participant book and should read the Introduction, How to Use This Book, and Chapter 1: Focus on the Basics. Because not all participants will have an opportunity to read the corresponding chapters in preparation for each session, it will be important for you as the leader to summarize as you move through the discussion using the helps included in this guide. This will allow everyone to participate fully.

## ABOUT THE PARTICIPANT BOOK

This study has been created especially for busy people with many demands on their time. The chapters in the participant book are short and readable, with highlighted subtitles for a quick summary of topics. At the end of each chapter, readers will find a Reflect section to record their thoughts in response to specific questions. Drawing on the imagery of athletes who train for sporting events, they will be guided by the following:

##  A Disciple's Playbook

A playbook is a notebook with strategies and diagrams, usually used to outline the execution of football plays. For Christians, the playbook is the Bible. This is the place from which all our study and inquiry begins. Each chapter is based on a passage of Scripture. A question at the end of each chapter in the Disciple's Playbook section will invite group members to reflect further on the Scripture passage.

##  Game Plan

A game plan refers to a strategy in sports, politics, or business that has been worked out in advance. This section invites group members to reflect on the insights they gained from each section of the chapter and record the learnings that are significant for them. This game plan is designed to help make practical applications for daily living.

## Score

A score refers to the number of points a player or team has earned in a game. This section invites group members to share the "winning point" from this chapter. What was most memorable about the chapter for you? Was it a passage of Scripture, a certain story, or special statement? This is an opportunity to write down the take-away received from reading the chapter.

Encourage participants to complete each of these three items in the Reflect section of their books, explaining that this will prepare them for the group discussion.

## About This Leader Guide

This leader guide is designed to assist you in expedient planning for the group sessions. Four session guides are included, each having a suggested format of 45 to 60 minutes. Additional optional activities are provided to extend the time if needed or desired. Feel free to adapt the format and/or select activities as you wish to tailor the material for the needs of your particular group, making the study your own. You are encouraged to review the guide for each session and use the space provided to create your own plan and write notes.

Here is a brief overview of the elements included in the session guide:

### Leader Prep (Before the Session)

For your preparation prior to the group session, this section includes a list of materials needed; a summary of the main idea of the session; the session goals; a biblical foundation or focus Scripture(s), along with brief commentary about the passage(s); and additional Scriptures that give further insights and support to the biblical themes of the session.

## Group Session Guide

### Welcome/Opening Prayer (5 minutes)

Welcome participants and have everyone introduce themselves if there are newcomers present. Offer a prayer of your own, or use the one provided. You also may wish to invite a group member to pray. Prayer requests may be shared at this time or at the end of the session.

## Opening Activity (5 minutes)

Begin the session with an icebreaker introduction to the discussion—a question to put the group at ease and get the conversation going.

## Reflect (25–40 minutes)

This portion of the session relates to the Reflect section at the end of the chapter. You will want to encourage participants to refer to that section of the book during this time as you cover A Disciple's Playbook, Game Plan, and Score.

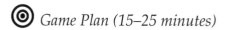 *A Disciple's Playbook (5–10 minutes)*

Read the Scripture aloud and offer background information to provide context for the lesson.

 *Game Plan (15–25 minutes)*

This section guides you in focusing on the main insights from the chapter. Present the summary of each section of the chapter, reading the material provided or summarizing it in your own words, and then select from the questions provided to lead discussion of the main points. Material for practical application is provided as well.

🏁 *Score (5 minutes)*

Next you will invite group members to share their main take-away—what they will remember most from this lesson.

## Wrap Up (5 minutes)

Now it's time to look ahead to next week. Introduce the next chapter briefly and allow time for prayer requests and other announcements.

## Closing Prayer (5 minutes)

Conclude the session with prayer. Offer an original prayer, praying specifically for any prayer requests, or pray the prayer provided. You also may invite one of the group members to pray or ask the group to pray "The Lord's Prayer" together (Matthew 6:9-13).

## Extra Material for an Extended Session

Each session guide is followed by additional activities and discussion questions to give you more options in designing the session. This additional material can be used to extend discussion by 15 to 30 minutes. It also serves as a quick go-to resource if the session is running ahead of schedule and you need to fill more time.

— — — — — — — — — — — — — —

It is our prayer that this study will bring encouragement and inspiration to all who long to get off the sidelines and get in the game. May God bless you as you lead others to deeper faith in our Lord and Savior, Jesus Christ.

# TIPS FOR FACILITATING A SMALL GROUP

- As you prepare for each session, pray for God's guidance. Pray for the participants by name—that each will receive from the study a message to deepen his or her faith as a follower of Jesus.
- Arrive at your meeting place several minutes early to prepare the room. If necessary, rearrange the chairs so participants will be comfortable and able to see each other during the discussion. Small touches such as beverages, refreshments, mints, tissue boxes, and so forth can help create an atmosphere of hospitality and welcome. Your enthusiasm for the opportunity to come together for fellowship and study will set the tone for a positive experience!
- Welcome participants as they arrive. Introduce newcomers and help them get acquainted with others.

- If appropriate, pass around pen and paper in your first session for participants to record their contact information. Seek permission of the group to send a weekly e-mail reminder about the upcoming session, as well as prayer requests that have been shared.
- Ask participants to bring their Bibles to each session. If possible, provide extra Bibles to share with those who did not bring them.
- Make sure everyone has a copy of the book and a pen or pencil.
- Start the session on time.
- As a part of either the opening or closing prayers, invite participants to share prayer requests.
- Throughout the session, include others by inviting them to read Scripture or sections of the chapter, lead in prayer, and so forth. You can simply ask: "Would someone please read/pray?"
- Establish a climate of mutual respect and acceptance that allows each person to share honestly.
- Model openness for sharing by being willing to respond to questions first if no one else does.
- Give gentle reminders regarding time, the amount of material left to cover, and so forth to keep the conversation going forward and to discourage one person from dominating the discussion.
- Encourage everyone's participation by offering positive affirmations for responses and asking further questions to help deepen the discussion.
- At the end of the session, invite participants to the next session by noting the next chapter title.
- End the session with prayer—and end on time! Express gratitude for everyone's attendance and participation in the discussion.

# FOCUS ON THE BASICS

## Leader Prep

### Materials Needed

- *Get in the Game* books and Bibles (participants should read Chapter 1 prior to the session)
- Pens and pencils
- Board or chart paper and marker (optional activity)

### Main Idea

What's the most important commandment? Jesus said it clearly, "Love God with all your heart, soul, and mind," and "love your neighbor as yourself" (Matthew 22:37, 39). So what does it mean for us to put this into practice as followers of Christ?

## Session Goals

This session is intended to help participants:

- Embrace a relationship with God that is dynamic and growing.
- Focus on Jesus' commandment to love God and neighbor.

## Biblical Foundation

³⁴*When the Pharisees heard that he had silenced the Sadducees, they gathered together,* ³⁵*and one of them, a lawyer, asked him a question to test him.* ³⁶*"Teacher, which commandment in the law is the greatest?"* ³⁷*He said to him, "'You shall love the Lord your God with all your heart, and with all your soul, and with all your mind.'* ³⁸*This is the greatest and first commandment.* ³⁹*And a second is like it: 'You shall love your neighbor as yourself.'* ⁴⁰*On these two commandments hang all the law and the prophets."*

*(Matthew 22:34-40)*

In this Scripture passage, Jesus summarizes all of the 613 laws of the Torah, the first five books of the Bible, into one compelling commandment: Love God with everything in your being, and love your neighbor as yourself. Jesus was taking two teachings found among the 613. First, he was referencing what is known as the Shema, one of the most important sayings of the Jewish people found in Deuteronomy 6:4-5: "Hear, O Israel: The LORD is God, the LORD alone. You shall love the LORD your God with all your heart, and with all your soul, and with all your might."

This law was what separated the Hebrew people from other cultures in the world at the time, many of whom were polytheistic. That is, they worshiped many gods. The Jewish people believed fiercely in the idea that there is but one true God, and God alone is to be worshiped.

The second law Jesus was drawing on is found in Leviticus 19:18: "You shall not take vengeance or bear a grudge against any of your people, but you shall love your neighbor as yourself." Jesus explains that everything that is written in the law and the prophets hang on these two sayings. The challenge of this is translating one's love of God into a love for neighbor. Because you love God, you strive to love your neighbor as yourself.

In Luke's version of this story (Luke 10:25-37), the lawyer pushes the issue and asks the question, "And who is my neighbor?" In response, Jesus tells the story of the good Samaritan. What does it mean for us to show compassion to others? How can we make the love we have for God more tangible? What does loving our neighbor look like in action? What does loving myself have to do with loving God and neighbor? All of these questions and more confront us in this great commandment. Love God and love neighbor, as we love ourselves.

*Note for leaders:* You may want to take the members of your group into a sampling of the 613 laws. Reading Deuteronomy 24 would give your group a good example of how there were laws for all kinds of different issues people faced.

## Additional Scriptures

*4Hear, O Israel: The LORD is our God, the LORD alone. 5You shall love the LORD your God with all your heart, and with all your soul, and with all your might. 6Keep these words that I am commanding you today in your heart. 7Recite them to your children and talk about them when you are at home and when you are away, when you lie down and when you rise. 8Bind them as a sign on your hand, fix them as an emblem on your forehead, 9and write them on the doorposts of your house and on your gates.*

*(Deuteronomy 6:4-9)*

*34I give you a new commandment, that you love one another. Just as I have loved you, you also should love one another. 35By this everyone will know that you are my disciples, if you have love for one another."*

*(John 13:34-35)*

*8Owe no one anything, except to love one another; for the one who loves another has fulfilled the law. 9The commandments, "You shall not commit adultery; You shall not murder; You shall not steal; You shall not covet"; and any other commandment, are summed up in this word, "Love your neighbor as yourself." 10Love does no wrong to a neighbor; therefore, love is the fulfilling of the law.*

*(Romans 13:8-10)*

*For the whole law is summed up in a single commandment, "You shall love your neighbor as yourself."*

*(Galatians 5:14)*

*1Then God spoke all these words:*
*2I am the LORD your God, who brought you out of the land of*

*Egypt, out of the house of slavery;* <sup>3</sup>*you shall have no other gods before me.*

<sup>4</sup>*You shall not make for yourself an idol, whether in the form of anything that is in heaven above, or that is on the earth beneath, or that is in the water under the earth.* <sup>5</sup>*You shall not bow down to them or worship them; for I the* Lord *your God am a jealous God, punishing children for the iniquity of parents, to the third and the fourth generation of those who reject me,* <sup>6</sup>*but showing steadfast love to the thousandth generation of those who love me and keep my commandments.*

<sup>7</sup>*You shall not make wrongful use of the name of the* Lord *your God, for the* Lord *will not acquit anyone who misuses his name.*

<sup>8</sup>*Remember the sabbath day, and keep it holy.* <sup>9</sup>*Six days you shall labor and do all your work.* <sup>10</sup>*But the seventh day is a sabbath to the* Lord *your God; you shall not do any work—you, your son or your daughter, your male or female slave, your livestock, or the alien resident in your towns.* <sup>11</sup>*For in six days the* Lord *made heaven and earth, the sea, and all that is in them, but rested the seventh day; therefore the* Lord *blessed the sabbath day and consecrated it.*

<sup>12</sup>*Honor your father and your mother, so that your days may be long in the land that the* Lord *your God is giving you.*

<sup>13</sup>*You shall not murder.*

<sup>14</sup>*You shall not commit adultery.*

<sup>15</sup>*You shall not steal.*

<sup>16</sup>*You shall not bear false witness against your neighbor.*

<sup>17</sup>*You shall not covet your neighbor's house; you shall not covet your neighbor's wife, or male or female slave, or ox, or donkey, or anything that belongs to your neighbor.*

*(Exodus 20:1-17)*

# Session Guide

## Welcome/Opening Prayer (5 minutes)

Welcome participants and make introductions, if necessary. You may wish to begin with prayer requests to include in the opening prayer, or you may save these for the closing prayer time. Note that today's session is the first of a four-part series and that you will be covering the content from Chapter 1 of *Get in the Game*. If appropriate, pass around a sign-up sheet to gather contact information. Seek permission of the group to set up a group e-mail so that you can send a weekly reminder about the chapter you will be studying, as well as prayer requests.

Now lead the group in an opening prayer, or ask a participant to pray. You may use your own prayer or the one below:

*Almighty God, thank you for this day and the opportunity to be in your presence and study your Word. Open our hearts and minds as we gather here. We want to walk with you and be your people. We love you, Lord, and we want to please you. As we put our faith in you, we ask you to direct our path in the way we should go. In Jesus' name we pray. Amen.*

## Opening Activity (5 minutes)

To introduce the study, read or ask a participant to read the Introduction in *Get in the Game*, pages 11–13.

## Reflect (25–40 minutes)

As you begin the Reflect section, review and explain the three terms: A Disciple's Playbook, Game Plan, and Score (see pages 15–17, "How to Use This Book," in *Get in the Game*). You will want to encourage participants to refer to the Reflect section at the end of the chapter during this time.

### ✗ *A Disciple's Playbook (5–10 minutes)*

Read or ask a group member to read Matthew 22: 34-40, and the contextual background of this Scripture reading, found on pages 38–39 of *Get in the Game*. You may wish to share more background about this particular Scripture (see Biblical Foundation, pages 14–15 of this Leader Guide).

Ask group members to share their response to the question in this section:

- What is the most practical way to show my love for God and neighbor?

### ◎ *Game Plan (15–25 minutes)*

Summarize each of the sections below, pausing after each summary to ask group members to share the insights they listed in their books. Discuss why the insights were significant to them, and ask how these insights will be applied in daily living.

- *Growing in Christ*

Summary: Living in a relationship with God means that you take intentional steps day by day, growing toward the person that God imagines you to be. You allow God to forgive you, shape you, mold you, and make you into the best version of yourself. As a follower of Jesus, you are growing in grace.

Other notes:

Discuss the following:

- What insights did you record in your books?
- Why were these insights significant to you?
- How can you apply these insights in your daily living?

- *Jesus Gives Two Commandments*

Summary: It is interesting to note that of the 613 laws in the Torah, 248 were "positive" commandments, and 365 were "negative" commandments. If one really wanted to live the law, he or she would be expected to follow these commandments, 365 days a year, with all of his or her being. Though that standard is humanly impossible, it's important to note that all of the 613 laws hang on these two: Love God, and love your neighbor as yourself.

Other notes:

Discuss the following:

- What insights did you record in your books?
- Why were these insights significant to you?
- How can you apply these insights in your daily living?

- *Love God*

Summary: Because we love God, we are invited into a relationship with God that is growing and evolving. God challenges us to put our fear behind, to live in faith, and to move forward in our lives.

Other notes:

Discuss the following:

- What insights did you record in your books?
- Why were these insights significant to you?
- How can you apply these insights in your daily living?

- *Loving Our Neighbor as We Love Ourselves*

Summary: We are called to be loving toward our neighbors, to treat our neighbors as we would want to be treated. Jesus summed it up: everything in the law is about loving God and loving neighbor. And he had one more thing to say that is often overlooked—love yourself, because you are a dearly beloved child of God.

Other notes:

Discuss the following:

- What insights did you record in your books?
- Why were these insights significant to you?
- How can you apply these insights in your daily living?

- *Get in the Game*

Summary: Are you ready to get off of the sidelines and get into the game? Are you ready to commit today to growing in your relationship with God, with your neighbors, and with yourself?

Other notes:

Discuss the following:

- What insights did you record in your books?
- Why were these insights significant to you?
- How can you apply these insights in your daily living

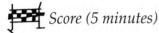 *Score (5 minutes)*

Invite participants to share their answers to the question *What's the "winning point" you will remember from this chapter?*

and tell why this was especially meaningful to them. Be prepared to share your own answer first if necessary.

## Wrap Up (5 minutes)

Ask participants to turn to Chapter 2: Get in the Zone (page 41). Say: "Our next session will focus on Romans 12:1-8," and offer any additional comments you would like to make about the focus of the next session. Let group members know that you look forward to your next time of study and prayer together. This also is a good time to communicate any announcements or group housekeeping details that need to be shared with the group.

## Closing Prayer (5 minutes)

Lead the group in prayer. You may pray the one provided below, offer one of your own, or invite a participant to pray. If prayer requests were shared at the beginning, remind the group to include these in their daily prayer time in the coming week. Or invite prayer requests at this time and include them in the prayer. Another option is to invite everyone to recite the Lord's Prayer (Matthew 6:9-13).

*Gracious and loving God, we thank you for this time together. Too often our lives are so consumed with the accessories that we forget the basics. Help us to love you with all of our hearts, souls, and minds. And help us to put our love for you in action, by loving our neighbors as we love ourselves. Send us out into the world to love your people. In Jesus' name. Amen.*

## Extra Material for an Extended Session

### Extra Activities

- Read or ask a participant to read Deuteronomy 24. Note the various laws for all kinds of different issues people faced in biblical times.
- Ask participants to look up and read Scriptures included in the Additional Scriptures section. You may wish to write the list of Scriptures on a chalkboard or on individual pieces of paper to distribute.

### Extra Discussion Questions

- What makes the greatest difference for you in growing your relationship with God?
- How do you find ways to refocus on priorities when you are feeling overwhelmed?

---

## Notes for the Session

## Session 2

# GET IN THE ZONE

## Leader Prep

### Materials Needed

- *Get in the Game* books and Bibles
- Pens and pencils
- Board or chart paper and marker (optional activity)

### Main Idea

Athletes practice over and over until that which is challenging becomes almost routine. In a similar way, disciples are called to get in "the zone" with God. The challenge is to not be conformed to others' expectations, but to be transformed by the love of God.

## Session Goals

This session is intended to help participants:

- Consider the spiritual disciplines that align our lives with God's will.
- Recognize the ways we open ourselves to being transformed by God.
- Reflect on the gifts we've been given and how we can best use them to serve God.

## Biblical Foundation

*¹I appeal to you therefore, brothers and sisters, by the mercies of God, to present your bodies as a living sacrifice, holy and acceptable to God, which is your spiritual worship. ²Do not be conformed to this world, but be transformed by the renewing of your minds, so that you may discern what is the will of God—what is good and acceptable and perfect.*

*³For by the grace given to me I say to everyone among you not to think of yourself more highly than you ought to think, but to think with sober judgment, each according to the measure of faith that God has assigned. ⁴For as in one body we have many members, and not all the members have the same function, ⁵so we, who are many, are one body in Christ, and individually we are members one of another. ⁶We have gifts that differ according to the grace given to us: prophecy, in proportion to faith; ⁷ministry, in ministering; the teacher, in teaching; ⁸the exhorter, in exhortation; the giver, in generosity; the leader, in diligence; the compassionate, in cheerfulness.*

*(Romans 12:1-8)*

Paul gives us a wonderful outline for living in the God Zone, for living a life in sync with what God would have us do. The first verses of Romans 12 are filled with instruction for us. Paul is telling us we have to give ourselves fully to God, invest ourselves fully. Being a Christian is about being "all in" and fully committed.

What is Paul saying to the people? God did not ask them for an animal sacrifice. In the Old Testament we often read about people bringing an animal to sacrifice before the Lord as a way to be forgiven for various sins and transgressions (see Genesis 4:4-5). They understood this sacrifice as a symbolic act of atonement to right themselves with God. But now, because of what Jesus, the Lamb of God, has done for us on the cross, animal sacrifice is no longer necessary (see Hebrews 7:27). Instead, Paul urges our very lives to become a living sacrifice, to put God's agenda ahead of our own.

Paul then encourages followers of Christ in Romans 12:2 to "not be conformed to this world, but...transformed by the renewing of your minds." Christians are challenged to be distinguishable from the rest of the world, not adopting the values of the world, but staying connected to Christ. Through this connection God does the work of transformation, changing our minds, our thoughts, and our internal conversations to more closely mirror the mind of Christ. This internal conversation shapes our thoughts and actions over time, enabling us to have greater discernment about what God would have us do.

Being more closely aligned with God's will, we are then challenged in Romans 12:3-8 to consider, "with sober judgment," how our gifts can be used in God's mission. We are part of the body of Christ, an image Paul also uses in

1 Corinthians 12. We all have different gifts and should use those gifts as we have been so blessed. The question every Christian must answer is, "What gifts do I have that can best serve the cause of Christ?" It is also critical to remember that every person has gifts and they are not the same. Yet, we all are part of the one body. How can we honor the gifts of each member of the body, as we strive together to do what is pleasing to God?

## Additional Scriptures

> [6]*"With what shall I come before the Lord,*
> *and bow myself before God on high?*
> *Shall I come before him with burnt offerings,*
> *with calves a year old?*
> [7]*Will the Lord be pleased with thousands of rams,*
> *with ten thousands of rivers of oil?*
> *Shall I give my firstborn for my transgression,*
> *the fruit of my body for the sin of my soul?"*
> [8]*He has told you, O mortal, what is good;*
> *and what does the Lord require of you*
> *but to do justice, and to love kindness,*
> *and to walk humbly with your God?*
>
> (Micah 6:6-8)

[12]*As God's chosen ones, holy and beloved, clothe yourselves with compassion, kindness, humility, meekness, and patience.* [13]*Bear with one another and, if anyone has a complaint against another, forgive each other; just as the Lord has forgiven you, so you also must forgive.* [14]*Above all, clothe yourselves with love, which binds everything together in perfect harmony.* [15]*And let the peace of Christ rule in your hearts, to which indeed you*

were called in the one body. And be thankful. [16]Let the word of Christ dwell in you richly; teach and admonish one another in all wisdom; and with gratitude in your hearts sing psalms, hymns, and spiritual songs to God. [17]And whatever you do, in word or deed, do everything in the name of the Lord Jesus, giving thanks to God the Father through him.

(Colossians 3:12-17)

[4]Now there are varieties of gifts, but the same Spirit; [5]and there are varieties of services, but the same Lord; [6]and there are varieties of activities, but it is the same God who activates all of them in everyone. [7]To each is given the manifestation of the Spirit for the common good. [8]To one is given through the Spirit the utterance of wisdom, and to another the utterance of knowledge according to the same Spirit, [9]to another faith by the same Spirit, to another gifts of healing by the one Spirit, [10]to another the working of miracles, to another prophecy, to another the discernment of spirits, to another various kinds of tongues, to another the interpretation of tongues. [11]All these are activated by one and the same Spirit, who allots to each one individually just as the Spirit chooses.

[12]For just as the body is one and has many members, and all the members of the body, though many, are one body, so it is with Christ. [13]For in the one Spirit we were all baptized into one body— Jews or Greeks, slaves or free—and we were all made to drink of one Spirit.

[14]Indeed, the body does not consist of one member but of many. [15]If the foot would say, "Because I am not a hand, I do not belong to the body," that would not make it any less a part of the body. [16]And if the ear would say, "Because I am not an eye, I do not belong to the body," that would not make it any less a part of the body. [17]If the whole body were an eye, where would the hearing be?

If the whole body were hearing, where would the sense of smell be? [18]But as it is, God arranged the members in the body, each one of them, as he chose. [19]If all were a single member, where would the body be? [20]As it is, there are many members, yet one body. [21]The eye cannot say to the hand, "I have no need of you," nor again the head to the feet, "I have no need of you." [22]On the contrary, the members of the body that seem to be weaker are indispensable, [23]and those members of the body that we think less honorable we clothe with greater honor, and our less respectable members are treated with greater respect; [24]whereas our more respectable members do not need this. But God has so arranged the body, giving the greater honor to the inferior member, [25]that there may be no dissension within the body, but the members may have the same care for one another. [26]If one member suffers, all suffer together with it; if one member is honored, all rejoice together with it.

[27]Now you are the body of Christ and individually members of it. [28]And God has appointed in the church first apostles, second prophets, third teachers; then deeds of power, then gifts of healing, forms of assistance, forms of leadership, various kinds of tongues. [29]Are all apostles? Are all prophets? Are all teachers? Do all work miracles? [30]Do all possess gifts of healing? Do all speak in tongues? Do all interpret? [31]But strive for the greater gifts. And I will show you a still more excellent way.

(1 Corinthians 12:4-31)

## Session Guide

### Welcome/Opening Prayer (5 minutes)

Welcome participants and make introductions, if necessary. You may wish to begin with prayer requests to include in the opening prayer, or you may save these for the closing prayer time.

Lead the group in an opening prayer, or ask a participant to pray. You may use your own prayer or the one below:

*O God, you are the living Lord who calls us to life. Thank you for this day. Open us to know you are with us. We love you, Lord, and we want to do what you would have us do. We offer our lives to you today, and ask for your blessings upon us. As we study your Word today, help us not be conformed to the world. Instead, transform our minds, that we may live in harmony with your desire. In Jesus' name we pray. Amen.*

## Opening Activity (5 minutes)

Ask participants to recall a sporting event or a musical or theatrical performance in which athletes or artists gave outstanding performances. What made this event so memorable? Did the athletes or artists seem to be "in the zone"?

## Reflect (25–40 minutes)

You will want to encourage participants to refer to the Reflect section at the end of the chapter during this time.

Ⴟ *A Disciple's Playbook (5–10 minutes)*

Read or ask a group member to read Romans 12:1-8, followed by the contextual background of this Scripture reading found on pages 59–60 of *Get in the Game*.

Ask group members to share their response to the questions in this section:

- What sacrifices have I made for God? What gifts have I used in serving God?

◎ *Game Plan (15–25 minutes)*

Summarize each of the sections below, pausing after each summary to ask group members to share the insights they listed in their books. Discuss why the insights were significant to them, and ask how these insights will be applied in daily living.

- *The Zone*

Summary: Being in the zone allows you to slow down and see things more clearly. It can happen in sports, and in our relationships as well. Sometimes there's a synchronicity in our relationships, where everything comes together in such a wonderful way—we are "in sync" with another person.

Other notes:

Discuss the following:

- What insights did you record in your books?
- Why were these insights significant to you?
- How can you apply these insights in your daily living?

- *Get in the "God Zone"*

  Summary: What God is asking of us is to have a changed heart, a heart fully devoted to living for God. Psalm 100:2 says "worship the Lord with gladness" or "serve the Lord with gladness." (NKJV) Our worship is our service to God and our service to God is our worship. It is our whole being engaged in living for God, seeking to be on the same page with God in all we do.

  Other notes:



  Discuss the following:

  - What insights did you record in your books?
  - Why were these insights significant to you?
  - How can you apply these insights in your daily living?

- *Transformed in the God Zone*

  Summary: In order to be transformed, you have to open yourself to transformation. In every situation, you seek to discern what God's will is. As we do this day by day, our lives are transformed. God's grace is shaping us and molding us so that we become more Christlike in our spirit and actions.

  Other notes:

Discuss the following:

- What insights did you record in your books?
- Why were these insights significant to you?
- How can you apply these insights in your daily living?

- *Living in the God Zone*

Summary: Read the "You might be living in the God Zone" list on pages 52–53 in *Get in the Game*.

Other notes:

Discuss the following:

- What insights did you record in your books?
- Why were these insights significant to you?
- How can you apply these insights in your daily living?

- *Serving in the God Zone*

Summary: We discover that we have gifts that God can use, and we honor that others also have gifts that are also important. The body of Christ only functions at its highest level when we are all striving together to be in the God Zone, honoring each other for the contributions each can make.

Other notes:

Discuss the following:

- What insights did you record in your books?
- Why were these insights significant to you?
- How can you apply these insights in your daily living?

- *Going Forward*

Paul's letter to the Romans challenges us in multiple ways: Each of us is called to put our whole selves in, to live sacrificially for God. We allow God to begin the work of transformation in our hearts and minds, refusing to be conformed to the world, and we are called to discover the gifts God has given us, considering how we can use these gifts in ministry to bless the world. God is calling us to life! May we claim it, live it, and invest in it.

Other notes:

Discuss the following:

- What insights did you record in your books?
- Why were these insights significant to you?

- How can you apply these insights in your daily living?

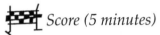 *Score (5 minutes)*

Invite participants to share their answers to the question *What's the "winning point" you will remember from this chapter?* and tell why this was especially meaningful to them. Be prepared to share your own answer first if necessary.

## Wrap Up (5 minutes)

Ask participants to turn to Chapter 3: Training (page 63). Say: "Our next session will focus on 1 Thessalonians 5:16-18 and Luke 17:11-19," and offer any additional comments you would like to make about the focus of the next session. Let group members know that you look forward to your next time of study and prayer together. This also is a good time to communicate any announcements or group housekeeping details that need to be shared with the group.

## Closing Prayer (5 minutes)

Lead the group in prayer. You may pray the one provided, offer one of your own, or invite a participant to pray. If prayer requests were shared at the beginning, remind the group to include these in their daily prayer time in the coming week. Or invite prayer requests at this time and include them in the prayer. Another option is to invite everyone to recite the Lord's Prayer (Matthew 6:9-13).

*Gracious and loving God, forgive us when we missed out on life because we have been too busy living. Remind us that you called us to a way of life that is unlike anything the world can offer us. In you we find true love, true meaning, true purpose, and true value. We pray, Lord, that somehow you might see us where we are, that as we open ourselves to you this day you might reveal to us your incredible love. Thank you for your gift of forgiveness, which sets us free so we might live in your zone; through Christ our Lord. Amen.*

# Extra Material for an Extended Session

## Extra Activities

- Prior to your session, ask participants to take a brief, online Spiritual Gifts Assessment (found at www.umc.org/what-we-believe/spiritual-gifts). Ask: "Were you surprised by the results? How might God be calling you to use your gifts?"
- Ask participants to look up and read Scriptures included in the Additional Scriptures section. You may wish to write the list of Scriptures on a chalkboard or on individual pieces of paper to distribute.

## Extra Discussion Questions

- When do you feel you are most "in sync" with God and God's will for your life?
- What service opportunity gives you the greatest joy?

# Notes for the Session

## Session 3

# TRAINING

### Leader Prep

## Materials Needed

- *Get in the Game* books and Bibles
- Pens and pencils
- Board or chart paper and marker (optional activity)

## Main Idea

Serving God and others comes through the intentional development of praise, prayer, and gratitude.

## Session Goals

This session is intended to help participants:

- Recognize the importance of offering praise to God in all circumstances.

- Understand prayer as relationship with God.
- Cultivate a "gratitude attitude" by practicing thankfulness.

## Biblical Foundation

[16]*Rejoice always,* [17]*pray without ceasing,* [18]*give thanks in all circumstances; for this is the will of God in Christ Jesus for you.*
(1 *Thessalonians 5:16-18*)

[11]*On the way to Jerusalem Jesus was going through the region between Samaria and Galilee.* [12]*As he entered a village, ten lepers approached him. Keeping their distance,* [13]*they called out, saying, "Jesus, Master, have mercy on us!"* [14]*When he saw them, he said to them, "Go and show yourselves to the priests." And as they went, they were made clean.* [15]*Then one of them, when he saw that he was healed, turned back, praising God with a loud voice.* [16]*He prostrated himself at Jesus' feet and thanked him. And he was a Samaritan.* [17]*Then Jesus asked, "Were not ten made clean? But the other nine, where are they?* [18]*Was none of them found to return and give praise to God except this foreigner?"* [19]*Then he said to him, "Get up and go on your way; your faith has made you well."*
(*Luke 17:11-19*)

First Thessalonians may be the earliest document in the New Testament. Paul is writing to those who have responded to the gospel message. Some of these believers evidently faced open hostility from those who rejected this message, as we read in 1 Thessalonians 1:6, "And you became imitators of us and of the Lord, for in spite of persecution you received the word with joy inspired by the Holy Spirit." In 1 Thessalonians 5:16-18, Paul directly appeals to God's will in terms of their proper behavior.

They are first called to "rejoice always." This closely mirrors Paul's encouragement to the church at Philippi, "Rejoice in the Lord, always; again I will say, Rejoice" (Philippians 4:4). Christians can rejoice always because of what God has done for us in the life, death, and resurrection of Jesus. Our situation may not be joyful, but God is a source of joy in all situations.

Paul also admonishes the believers to "pray without ceasing." Paul and his friends have indeed been doing this very thing for the Thessalonian believers, as he says in 1 Thessalonians 3:10: "Night and day we pray most earnestly that we may see you face to face and restore whatever is lacking in your faith." This is a word of encouragement to stay connected to God through every circumstance we face in life.

"Give thanks in all circumstances" completes these three sayings that Paul says are "the will of God in Christ Jesus for you." Being grateful is easy when all is well. Paul's challenge is to find gratitude in your heart, no matter what has happened. Again, because of what God has done for us in Jesus, we always have a reason to be grateful. Practicing gratitude is a spiritual discipline that opens us to understand God's desire for our lives. When we learn this behavior, it changes our lives, giving us a different perspective no matter what we are going through.

Luke's telling of Jesus and the ten lepers is a story unique to Luke's Gospel. Lepers were outcasts and could not come within a certain distance of healthy people. It had to do with both fear of the disease spreading and the cleansing rituals of being pure before God in order to be a part of the community. Lepers often had to beg for food, appealing to the compassion of strangers. Jesus is moved by their plight, has mercy upon them, and offers healing. As they go to show themselves to the priests, a step required to verify their health status, they all realize they have been healed. One stops to go back. Luke tells us he is a Samaritan. Jesus also lifts up a Samaritan as a positive role model in Luke 10:28-37. The Samaritans and Jews despised each other, a feud going back centuries, after the return from the Exile. That Luke uses another Samaritan in a positive light reminds us of the inclusive nature of God's love. Jesus came for all, not just the Hebrew people, but for the whole world. The invitation is for all.

Jesus says that the man who showed gratitude is made whole, another word for *salvation*. While the others are healed, there is a qualitative difference for the man who showed gratitude. Gratitude has that impact upon our lives. Many of us go through our lives and have amazing blessings. But how often do we truly stop and express gratitude for those blessings? Jesus lifts up the foreigner as the one who got it right. Living gratefully is a lifestyle and one that takes practice.

## Additional Scriptures

Rejoicing:

*Be glad in the Lord and rejoice, O righteous,*
*and shout for joy, all you upright in heart.*
*(Psalm 32:11)*

*Our heart is glad in him,*
*because we trust in his holy name.*
*(Psalm 33:21)*

*⁹As the Father has loved me, so I have loved you; abide in my love. ¹⁰If you keep my commandments, you will abide in my love, just as I have kept my Father's commandments and abide in his love. ¹¹I have said these things to you so that my joy may be in you, and that your joy may be complete.*

*¹²"This is my commandment, that you love one another as I have loved you."*

(John 15:9-12)

Praying:

*Seek the Lord and his strength,*
*  seek his presence continually.*
*    (1 Chronicles 16:11)*

*⁷ "Ask, and it will be given you; search, and you will find; knock, and the door will be opened for you. ⁸For everyone who asks receives, and everyone who searches finds, and for everyone who knocks, the door will be opened. ⁹Is there anyone among you who, if your child asks for bread, will give a stone? ¹⁰Or if the child asks for a fish, will give a snake? ¹¹If you then, who are evil, know how to give good gifts to your children, how much more will your Father in heaven give good things to those who ask him!"*

(Matthew 7:7-11)

*²⁶Likewise the Spirit helps us in our weakness; for we do not know how to pray as we ought, but that very Spirit intercedes with sighs too deep for words. ²⁷And God, who searches the heart, knows what is the mind of the Spirit, because the Spirit intercedes for the saints according to the will of God.*

*²⁸We know that all things work together for good for those who love God, who are called according to his purpose.*

(Romans 8:26-28)

Giving Thanks:

*O give thanks to the Lord, for he is good;*
*for his steadfast love endures forever.*

(*Psalm 107:1*)

*Every generous act of giving, with every perfect gift, is from above, coming down from the Father of lights, with whom there is no variation or shadow due to change.*

(*James 1:17*)

[3]*Grace to you and peace from God our Father and the Lord Jesus Christ.*

[4]*I give thanks to my God always for you because of the grace of God that has been given you in Christ Jesus, [5]for in every way you have been enriched in him, in speech and knowledge of every kind—[6]just as the testimony of Christ has been strengthened among you—[7]so that you are not lacking in any spiritual gift as you wait for the revealing of our Lord Jesus Christ.*

(*1 Corinthians 1:3-7*)

## Session Guide

### Welcome/Opening Prayer (5 minutes)

Welcome participants. You may wish to begin with prayer requests to include in the opening prayer, or you may save these for the closing prayer time.

Lead the group in an opening prayer, or ask a participant to pray. You may use your own prayer or the one below:

*Spirit of the living God, fall afresh upon us. We are grateful for our many blessings this day. We ask you to forgive our shortcomings. Help us train to do those things that will build up ourselves and others, and not tear each other down. Remind us that life is a gift, and we have an opportunity every day to respond to that gift with our lives. As we gather to study your Word today, speak to each one of us a word of life. Encourage our spirits, loving God, that we may be a source of blessing to the world you love. In Jesus' name we pray. Amen.*

## Opening Activity (5 minutes)

Ask participants to tell about a time they were surprised by someone expressing thanks and gratitude. How did it make them feel?

## Reflect (25–40 minutes)

You will want to encourage participants to refer to the Reflect section at the end of the chapter during this time.

## Ϫ *A Disciple's Playbook (5–10 minutes)*

Read or ask a group member to read 1 Thessalonians 5:16-18 and Luke 17:11-19, followed by the contextual background of this Scripture reading found on pages 82–84 of *Get in the Game*.

Ask group members to share their responses to the questions in this section:

- How can I train to rejoice, pray, and give thanks in all circumstances? Does my life look more like the one or more like the nine?

## ◎ *Game Plan (15–25 minutes)*

Summarize each of the sections below, pausing after each summary to ask group members to share the insights they listed in their books. Discuss why the insights were significant to them, and ask how these insights will be applied in daily living.

- *Rejoice Always*

Summary: Through difficult circumstances in our own lives, in the lives of others, and in the world, we are called to be those people who are finding reasons to rejoice. Because of what God has done for us in the life, death, and resurrection of Jesus, we can learn to rejoice always.

Other notes:

Discuss the following:

- What insights did you record in your books?
- Why were these insights significant to you?
- How can you apply these insights in your daily living?

- *Pray Without Ceasing*

Summary: Praying without ceasing isn't just about bowing our heads; it is about an ongoing conversation with the One who created us. Training ourselves to seek God, worship God, be aware of God, and call on God for help, reminds us that we have a relationship with the Source of strength, hope, and love.

Other notes:

Discuss the following:

- What insights did you record in your books?
- Why were these insights significant to you?
- How can you apply these insights in your daily living?

- *Give Thanks in All Circumstances*

Summary: Christians are those who are learning to be thankful for the blessings they have in the midst of good times and bad times. Luke teaches us something important about the Christian life: it's not just about following a set of rules. Although Christians don't dismiss the law, the Christian life should primarily be a response of gratitude, returning daily to the Source of blessing to express gratitude.

Other notes:

Discuss the following:

- What insights did you record in your book?
- Why were these insights significant to you?
- How can you apply these insights in your daily living?

- *Practical Training*

Summary: Making gratitude a holy habit not only changes us, it changes the people in the world around us. There are many people we appreciate in our hearts and minds. But have we expressed our thanks and appreciation? Have we told them so? What if we were intentional in expressing gratitude on an ongoing basis to our family, our friends, those we interact with every day, strangers we meet along the way, and especially to God?

Other notes:

Discuss the following:

- What insights did you record in your book?

- Why were these insights significant to you?
- How can you apply these insights in your daily living?

- *Grateful to God*

Summary: We need to remember that before we can go forward to address our many daily responsibilities, we need to "go back" to God and say "thanks." We need to acknowledge our gratitude to God from whom all blessings flow, the Source and Center of our lives.

Other notes:

Discuss the following:

- What insights did you record in your books?
- Why were these insights significant to you?
- How can you apply these insights in your daily living?

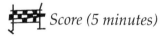 *Score (5 minutes)*

Invite participants to share their answers to the question *What's the "winning point" you will remember from this chapter?* and tell why this was especially meaningful to them. Be prepared to share your own answer first if necessary.

## Wrap Up (5 minutes)

Ask participants to turn to Chapter 4: All In: A Life of Generosity (page 87). Say: "Our next session will focus on 2 Corinthians 8:1-7; 9:7," and offer any additional comments you would like to make about the focus of the next session. Let group members know that you look forward to your next time of study and prayer together. This also is a good time to communicate any announcements or group housekeeping details that need to be shared with the group.

## Closing Prayer (5 minutes)

Lead the group in prayer. You may pray the one provided below, offer one of your own, or invite a participant to pray. If prayer requests were shared at the beginning, remind the group to include these in their daily prayer time in the coming week. Or invite prayer requests at this time and include them in the prayer. Another option is to invite everyone to recite the Lord's Prayer (Matthew 6:9-13).

*Lord, we want so desperately for our lives to reflect what we experienced of your grace, your love, and your mercy. To let our lives shine in such a way that others begin to see the gratitude with which we live. When they ask why we're so grateful, we will tell them, Lord, it's because we have been blessed by you, the Source of all of life. We thank you for all your gifts, Christ our Lord. In Jesus' name we pray, Amen.*

# Extra Material for an Extended Session

## Extra Activities

- Pass out paper and pencils or pens. Ask participants to write down five things for which they are grateful. Then ask them to write down the names of seven people to whom they will write thank-you notes. Encourage them to follow up by writing down five things each day for which they are grateful, as well as writing one thank-you note each day of the coming week.
- Ask participants to look up and read Scriptures from the Additional Scriptures section. You may wish to write the list of Scriptures on a chalkboard or on individual pieces of paper to distribute.

## Extra Discussion Questions

- How can you focus on finding more joy in your everyday life? How can you help others experience a more joyful life?
- What would happen in our lives if we focused more on our relationship with God throughout the day?
- What would our lives be like if we could cultivate a "gratitude attitude"? What difference could we make in the lives of others if our gratitude attitude became contagious?

# Notes for the Session

# ALL IN

## A Life of Generosity

### Leader Prep

**Materials Needed**

- *Get in the Game* books and Bibles
- Pens and pencils
- Board or chart paper and marker (optional activity)

**Main Idea**

Paul tells us about the poverty-stricken churches of Macedonia, who begged for the privilege of participating in an offering. Throughout the ages followers of Christ have demonstrated generosity as one of the marks of discipleship, yet many Christians are reluctant to talk about monetary giving. The Bible has many teachings on living a life of generosity.

## Session Goals

This session is intended to help participants:

- Understand the depth of God's generosity, given through the life, death, and resurrection of Jesus Christ.
- Reflect on the ways to respond to God's gift through the giving of all that we are and all that we have.
- Recognize that the spirit of our giving is more important than the amount of our gift.

## Biblical Foundation

*[8:1]We want you to know, brothers and sisters, about the grace of God that has been granted to the churches of Macedonia; [2]for during a severe ordeal of affliction, their abundant joy and their extreme poverty have overflowed in a wealth of generosity on their part. [3]For, as I can testify, they voluntarily gave according to their means, and even beyond their means, [4]begging us earnestly for the privilege of sharing in this ministry to the saints—[5]and this, not merely as we expected; they gave themselves first to the Lord and, by the will of God, to us, [6]so that we might urge Titus that, as he had already made a beginning, so he should also complete this generous undertaking among you. [7]Now as you excel in everything—in faith, in speech, in knowledge, in utmost eagerness, and in our love for you—so we want you to excel also in this generous undertaking....*

*[9:7]Each of you must give as you have made up your mind, not reluctantly or under compulsion, for God loves a cheerful giver.*

*(2 Corinthians 8:1-7; 9:7)*

One of the aspects of Paul's missionary journeys, recorded in the Book of Acts and revealed in some of his letters, is the relief offering for the saints in the mother church in Judea. The offering is first mentioned in Acts 11:27-30 and is referenced in Romans 15:26, among other places. The extreme poverty that Paul finds when he arrives in Macedonia makes him conclude that he will not ask these believers to be a part of this offering. However, perhaps because of their own experience of God's provision and grace, they have an "abundance of joy" that overflows into a "wealth of generosity." They may not have been able to give much, but they were overjoyed to offer what they could. They lived their faith as a response of gratitude for what God had done for them.

These Christians begged for an opportunity to bless the lives of others. For Christians this becomes a way of life. Generosity with possessions, money, time, and talent are not unusual expressions for those who have been set free by the grace of God. They are now freed from any reluctance to hold on to their things. They see themselves as stewards of what God has given to them. Helping others in need becomes a way of life. They give cheerfully, and God loves the spirit of cheerful giving. This raises good questions to ponder. Is my giving done reluctantly, under compulsion, or cheerfully? Do I see what I have as my own, or does it all belong to God? How am I being faithful as a steward or manager of what God has entrusted to me?

## Additional Scriptures

*In all this I have given you an example that by such work we must support the weak, remembering the words of the Lord Jesus, for he himself said, "It is more blessed to give than to receive."*

*(Acts 20:35)*

*⁹Honor the Lord with your substance*
*and with the first fruits of all your produce;*
*¹⁰then your barns will be filled with plenty,*
*and your vats will be bursting with wine.*

*(Proverbs 3:9-10)*

*Some give freely, yet grow all the richer;*
*others withhold what is due, and only suffer want.*

*(Proverbs 11:24)*

*¹⁹"Do not store up for yourselves treasures on earth, where moth and rust consume and where thieves break in and steal; ²⁰but store up for yourselves treasures in heaven, where neither moth nor rust consumes and where thieves do not break in and steal. ²¹For where your treasure is, there your heart will be also."*

*(Matthew 6:19-21)*

*³⁷"Do not judge, and you will not be judged; do not condemn, and you will not be condemned. Forgive, and you will be forgiven; ³⁸give, and it will be given to you. A good measure, pressed down, shaken together, running over, will be put into your lap; for the measure you give will be the measure you get back."*

*(Luke 6:37-38)*

## Session Guide

### Welcome/Opening Prayer (5 minutes)

Welcome participants. You may wish to begin with prayer requests to include in the opening prayer, or you may save these for the closing prayer time.

Lead the group in an opening prayer, or ask a participant to pray. You may use your own prayer or the one below:

*O God, you are the Source of all life. All that we have comes from you, and all of it belongs to you. Help us to understand our role as stewards of your creation. We offer our lives to you today, and we want to be all in as your followers. As we study your Word, guide us in how to live our lives. Give us the joy and privilege of participating in the work you are doing to bring light and love to the world, through Jesus Christ our Lord. In Jesus' name. Amen.*

## Opening Activity (5 minutes)

Ask participants to recall a time when they were the recipients of a very generous act, perhaps one that was an unexpected surprise. How did it make them feel?

## Reflect (25–40 minutes)

You will want to encourage participants to refer to the Reflect section at the end of the chapter during this time.

### Ӿ *A Disciple's Playbook (5–10 minutes)*

Read or ask a group member to read 2 Corinthians 8:1-7; 9:7, followed by the contextual background of these Scripture readings found on page 106 of *Get in the Game*. You may wish to share more background about these particular Scriptures (see Biblical Foundation, pages 54–55 of this Leader Guide).

Ask group members to share their response to the questions in this section:

- What would it mean for me to give myself first to the Lord? How can I be more generous with my time, talents, and treasure?

## ◎ *Game Plan (15–25 minutes)*

Summarize each of the sections below, pausing after each summary to ask group members to share the insights they listed in their books. Discuss why the insights were significant to them, and ask how these insights will be applied in daily living.

- *The "Want To" Spirit*

Summary: Throughout Paul's letters, as you follow his travels in the New Testament, he is taking up a relief offering for the saints at the Jerusalem church. This is first mentioned by Luke, the writer of Luke and Acts, in Acts 11:27-30. The Jerusalem church was the mother church and it had fallen on hard times. So as Paul preached at different churches and synagogues, he would ask them to give a love offering, a relief offering, for the saints at Jerusalem. He wasn't even going to ask the church at Macedonia to participate in the relief offering because of their extreme poverty. But they came to him and surprised him by begging for the opportunity.

Paul saw that the churches of Macedonia really wanted to give, and he wanted to relay that to the Corinthian church. The Corinthian church had ability and wealth and all kinds of opportunities that the Macedonian church didn't have. But if the Macedonian church could do it, the Corinthian church could do it too.

Other notes:

Discuss the following:
- What insights did you record in your books?
- Why were these insights significant to you?
- How can you apply these insights in your daily living?

- *Generosity and Gratitude*

Summary: One way to think about faith is that it is a grateful response to the gift God has given us through Jesus, and this response encompasses our whole lives. It's not just the giving of our financial support; it also includes all that we have and all that we are.

Other notes:

Discuss the following:

- What insights did you record in your books?
- Why were these insights significant to you?
- How can you apply these insights in your daily living?

- *Giving Ourselves to the Lord*

Summary: When God becomes *the* priority, other things in life tend to take their place in a way that makes more sense. Some things fall by the wayside because we realize that, in the long run, they are not as important. Other things, still very important to us, tend to find their rightful place. They are important, but not our priority. We give ourselves first to the Lord.

Other notes:

Discuss the following:

- What insights did you record in your books?
- Why were these insights significant to you?
- How can you apply these insights in your daily living?

- *Cheerful Giving*

Summary: Our giving to God should come out of glad and generous hearts. God has been so good to us—that is why we give. We give to causes we believe in, causes where we see something compelling happening. We have a joy about giving, knowing we are helping make a difference.

Other notes:

Discuss the following:

- What insights did you record in your books?
- Why were these insights significant to you?
- How can you apply these insights in your daily living?

- *All In*

Summary: Truthfully, there are times when the thought of giving our lives, and everything we are, to Christ is a little overwhelming. But God has an imagination for what our world can be. By working with God, focusing on the basics, getting in the zone, training daily to follow God's will, and giving our lives—all in—to God, we can step closer toward that vision.

Other notes:

Discuss the following:

- What insights did you record in your books?
- Why were these insights significant to you?
- How can you apply these insights in your daily living?

 *Score (5 minutes)*

Invite participants to share their answers to the question *What is the "winning point" that you will remember most from this chapter?* and tell why this was especially meaningful to them. Be prepared to share your own answer first if necessary.

## Wrap Up (5 minutes)

As you come to the end of this study, thank the group for their participation over these four sessions. If you will be facilitating future studies (in The Basics series or another study), invite them to be a part and note the date when the study will begin.

## Closing Prayer (5 minutes)

Encourage group members to continue remembering one another and the prayer requests that have been shared in their prayers.

Lead the group in prayer. You may pray the one provided below, offer one of your own, or invite a participant to pray. If prayer requests were shared at the beginning, remind the group to include these in their daily prayer time in the coming week. Or invite prayer requests at this time and include them in the prayer. Another option is to invite everyone to recite the Lord's Prayer (Matthew 6:9-13).

*Almighty God, you have challenged us to get off the sidelines and get in the game. Thank you for loving us, forgiving us, and redeeming us so that we can be your people. Send us out into the world that we may cheerfully give our lives, what we have and who we are, to be a blessing to the world. Give us glad and generous hearts in all we do. In Jesus' name we pray. Amen.*

## Extra Material for an Extended Session

### Extra Activities

- Ask participants to identify ministries in your church and/or community that share the love of Christ with others. Would your group be willing to volunteer their time to serve together at one of these ministries? Would you be willing to take an offering to give to these ministries?
- Ask participants to look up and read Scriptures from the Additional Scriptures section. You may wish to write the list of Scriptures on a chalkboard or on individual pieces of paper to distribute.

### Extra Discussion Questions

- Have you ever felt God challenge you to expand your reach, to be a part of something bigger than yourself?
- What cause creates the "want to" spirit in you that stirs you to "want to" make a positive difference in the lives of others?

# Notes for the Session

CPSIA information can be obtained
at www.ICGtesting.com
Printed in the USA
LVOW04s1120120116

469939LV00004B/21/P